A Smile a Day: A Child's Daily Journal

Jenna Iverson

Order this book online at www.trafford.com
or email orders@trafford.com

Most Trafford titles are also available at major online book retailers.

Printed in the United States of America.

ISBN: 978-1-4269-5187-9 (sc)
ISBN: 978-1-4269-5188-6 (hc)
ISBN: 978-1-4269-5189-3 (e)

Library of Congress Control Number: 2010918810

Trafford rev. 01/20/2011

 www.trafford.com

North America & international
toll-free: 1 888 232 4444 (USA & Canada)
phone: 250 383 6864 ♦ fax: 812 355 4082

Today is:_____

The best part of my day was:

_____

_____

_____

_____

Something nice I did for someone today was:

_____

_____

_____

_____

Tonight I will pray for:

Because:

_____

_____

_____

_____

More about my day:

_____

_____

_____

_____

Today is:_____

The best part of my day was:

_____

_____

_____

_____

Something nice I did for someone today was:

_____

_____

_____

_____

Tonight I will pray for:

Because:

_____

_____

_____

_____

More about my day:

_____

_____

_____

_____

_____

Today is:_____

The best part of my day was:

_____

_____

_____

_____

Something nice I did for someone today was:

_____

_____

_____

_____

Tonight I will pray for:

Because:

_____

_____

_____

_____

More about my day:

_____

_____

_____

_____

_____

Today is:_____

The best part of my day was:

_____

_____

_____

_____

Something nice I did for someone today was:

_____

_____

_____

_____

Tonight I will pray for:

Because:

_____

_____

_____

_____

More about my day:

_____

_____

_____

_____

_____

Today is:_____

The best part of my day was:

_____

_____

_____

_____

Something nice I did for someone today was:

_____

_____

_____

_____

Tonight I will pray for:

Because:

_____

_____

_____

_____

More about my day:

_____

_____

_____

_____

_____

Today is:_____

The best part of my day was:

_____

_____

_____

_____

Something nice I did for someone today was:

_____

_____

_____

_____

Tonight I will pray for:

Because:

_____

_____

_____

_____

More about my day:

_____

_____

_____

_____

_____

Today is:_____

The best part of my day was:

_____

_____

_____

_____

Something nice I did for someone today was:

_____

_____

_____

_____

Tonight I will pray for:

Because:

_____

_____

_____

_____

More about my day:

_____

_____

_____

_____

_____

Today is:_____

The best part of my day was:

_____

_____

_____

_____

Something nice I did for someone today was:

_____

_____

_____

_____

Tonight I will pray for:

Because:

_____

_____

_____

_____

More about my day:

_____

_____

_____

_____

_____

Today is:_____

The best part of my day was:

_____

_____

_____

_____

Something nice I did for someone today was:

_____

_____

_____

_____

Tonight I will pray for:

Because:

_____

_____

_____

_____

More about my day:

_____

_____

_____

_____

Today is:_____

The best part of my day was:

_____

_____

_____

_____

Something nice I did for someone today was:

_____

_____

_____

_____

Tonight I will pray for:

Because:

_____

_____

_____

_____

More about my day:

_____

_____

_____

_____

Today is:_____

The best part of my day was:

_____

_____

_____

_____

Something nice I did for someone today was:

_____

_____

_____

_____

Tonight I will pray for:

Because:

_____

_____

_____

_____

More about my day:

_____

_____

_____

_____

_____

Today is:_____

The best part of my day was:

_____

_____

_____

_____

Something nice I did for someone today was:

_____

_____

_____

_____

Tonight I will pray for:

Because:

_____

_____

_____

_____

More about my day:

_____

_____

_____

_____

_____

Today is:_____

The best part of my day was:

_____

_____

_____

_____

Something nice I did for someone today was:

_____

_____

_____

_____

Tonight I will pray for:

Because:

_____

_____

_____

_____

More about my day:

_____

_____

_____

_____

_____

Today is:_____

The best part of my day was:

_____

_____

_____

_____

Something nice I did for someone today was:

_____

_____

_____

_____

Tonight I will pray for:

Because:

_____

_____

_____

_____

More about my day:

_____

_____

_____

_____

_____

Today is:_____

The best part of my day was:

_____

_____

_____

_____

Something nice I did for someone today was:

_____

_____

_____

_____

Tonight I will pray for:

Because:

_____

_____

_____

_____

More about my day:

_____

_____

_____

_____

Today is:_____

The best part of my day was:

_____

_____

_____

_____

Something nice I did for someone today was:

_____

_____

_____

_____

Tonight I will pray for:
Because:

_____

_____

_____

_____

More about my day:

_____

_____

_____

_____

Today is:_____

The best part of my day was:

_____

_____

_____

_____

Something nice I did for someone today was:

_____

_____

_____

_____

Tonight I will pray for:

Because:

_____

_____

_____

_____

More about my day:

_____

_____

_____

_____

Today is:_____

The best part of my day was:

_____

_____

_____

_____

Something nice I did for someone today was:

_____

_____

_____

_____

Tonight I will pray for:

Because:

_____

_____

_____

_____

More about my day:

_____

_____

_____

_____

_____

Today is:_____

The best part of my day was:

_____

_____

_____

_____

Something nice I did for someone today was:

_____

_____

_____

_____

Tonight I will pray for:

Because:

_____

_____

_____

_____

More about my day:

_____

_____

_____

_____

_____

Today is:_____

The best part of my day was:

_____

_____

_____

_____

Something nice I did for someone today was:

_____

_____

_____

_____

Tonight I will pray for:

Because:

_____

_____

_____

_____

More about my day:

_____

_____

_____

_____

Today is:_____

The best part of my day was:

_____

_____

_____

_____

Something nice I did for someone today was:

_____

_____

_____

_____

Tonight I will pray for:

Because:

_____

_____

_____

_____

More about my day:

_____

_____

_____

_____

_____

Today is:_____

The best part of my day was:

_____

_____

_____

_____

Something nice I did for someone today was:

_____

_____

_____

_____

Tonight I will pray for:

Because:

_____

_____

_____

_____

More about my day:

_____

_____

_____

_____

_____

Today is:_____

The best part of my day was:

_____

_____

_____

_____

Something nice I did for someone today was:

_____

_____

_____

_____

Tonight I will pray for:

Because:

_____

_____

_____

_____

More about my day:

_____

_____

_____

_____

Today is:_____

The best part of my day was:

_____

_____

_____

_____

Something nice I did for someone today was:

_____

_____

_____

_____

Tonight I will pray for:
Because:

_____

_____

_____

_____

More about my day:

_____

_____

_____

_____

_____

Today is:_____

The best part of my day was:

_____

_____

_____

_____

Something nice I did for someone today was:

_____

_____

_____

_____

Tonight I will pray for:

Because:

_____

_____

_____

_____

More about my day:

_____

_____

_____

_____

_____

Today is:_____

The best part of my day was:

_____

_____

_____

_____

Something nice I did for someone today was:

_____

_____

_____

_____

Tonight I will pray for:

Because:

_____

_____

_____

_____

More about my day:

_____

_____

_____

_____

Today is:_____

The best part of my day was:

_____

_____

_____

_____

Something nice I did for someone today was:

_____

_____

_____

_____

Tonight I will pray for:

Because:

_____

_____

_____

_____

More about my day:

_____

_____

_____

_____

_____

Today is:_____

The best part of my day was:

_____

_____

_____

_____

Something nice I did for someone today was:

_____

_____

_____

Tonight I will pray for:

Because:

_____

_____

_____

_____

More about my day:

_____

_____

_____

_____

_____

Today is:_____

The best part of my day was:

_____

_____

_____

_____

Something nice I did for someone today was:

_____

_____

_____

_____

Tonight I will pray for:

Because:

_____

_____

_____

_____

More about my day:

_____

_____

_____

_____

Today is:_____

The best part of my day was:

_____

_____

_____

_____

Something nice I did for someone today was:

_____

_____

_____

_____

Tonight I will pray for:

Because:

_____

_____

_____

_____

More about my day:

_____

_____

_____

_____

_____

Today is:_____

The best part of my day was:

_____

_____

_____

_____

Something nice I did for someone today was:

_____

_____

_____

_____

Tonight I will pray for:

Because:

_____

_____

_____

_____

More about my day:

_____

_____

_____

_____

Today is:_____

The best part of my day was:

_____

_____

_____

_____

Something nice I did for someone today was:

_____

_____

_____

_____

Tonight I will pray for:

Because:

_____

_____

_____

_____

More about my day:

_____

_____

_____

_____

Today is:_____

The best part of my day was:

_____

_____

_____

_____

Something nice I did for someone today was:

_____

_____

_____

_____

Tonight I will pray for:

Because:

_____

_____

_____

_____

More about my day:

_____

_____

_____

_____

_____

Today is:_____

The best part of my day was:

_____

_____

_____

_____

Something nice I did for someone today was:

_____

_____

_____

_____

Tonight I will pray for:

Because:

_____

_____

_____

_____

More about my day:

_____

_____

_____

_____

_____

Today is:_____

The best part of my day was:

_____
_____
_____
_____

Something nice I did for someone today was:

_____
_____
_____
_____

Tonight I will pray for:
Because:

_____
_____
_____
_____

More about my day:

_____
_____
_____
_____

Today is:_____

The best part of my day was:

_____

_____

_____

_____

Something nice I did for someone today was:

_____

_____

_____

_____

Tonight I will pray for:

Because:

_____

_____

_____

_____

More about my day:

_____

_____

_____

_____

_____

Today is:_____

The best part of my day was:

_____

_____

_____

_____

Something nice I did for someone today was:

_____

_____

_____

_____

Tonight I will pray for:

Because:

_____

_____

_____

_____

More about my day:

_____

_____

_____

_____

Today is:_____

The best part of my day was:

_____
_____
_____
_____

Something nice I did for someone today was:

_____
_____
_____
_____

Tonight I will pray for:
Because:

_____
_____
_____
_____

More about my day:

_____
_____
_____
_____
_____

Today is:_____

The best part of my day was:

_____

_____

_____

_____

Something nice I did for someone today was:

_____

_____

_____

_____

Tonight I will pray for:

Because:

_____

_____

_____

_____

More about my day:

_____

_____

_____

_____

Today is:_____

The best part of my day was:

_____

_____

_____

_____

Something nice I did for someone today was:

_____

_____

_____

_____

Tonight I will pray for:

Because:

_____

_____

_____

_____

More about my day:

_____

_____

_____

_____

_____

Today is:_____

The best part of my day was:

_____

_____

_____

_____

Something nice I did for someone today was:

_____

_____

_____

_____

Tonight I will pray for:

Because:

_____

_____

_____

_____

More about my day:

_____

_____

_____

_____

Today is:_____

The best part of my day was:

_____

_____

_____

_____

Something nice I did for someone today was:

_____

_____

_____

_____

Tonight I will pray for:

Because:

_____

_____

_____

_____

More about my day:

_____

_____

_____

_____

_____

Today is:_____

The best part of my day was:

_____

_____

_____

_____

Something nice I did for someone today was:

_____

_____

_____

_____

Tonight I will pray for:

Because:

_____

_____

_____

_____

More about my day:

_____

_____

_____

_____

Today is:_____

The best part of my day was:

_____

_____

_____

_____

Something nice I did for someone today was:

_____

_____

_____

_____

Tonight I will pray for:

Because:

_____

_____

_____

_____

More about my day:

_____

_____

_____

_____

Today is:_____

The best part of my day was:

_____

_____

_____

_____

Something nice I did for someone today was:

_____

_____

_____

_____

Tonight I will pray for:

Because:

_____

_____

_____

_____

More about my day:

_____

_____

_____

_____

Today is:_____

The best part of my day was:

_____

_____

_____

_____

Something nice I did for someone today was:

_____

_____

_____

_____

Tonight I will pray for:

Because:

_____

_____

_____

_____

More about my day:

_____

_____

_____

_____

_____

Today is:_____

The best part of my day was:

_____

_____

_____

_____

Something nice I did for someone today was:

_____

_____

_____

_____

Tonight I will pray for:

Because:

_____

_____

_____

_____

More about my day:

_____

_____

_____

_____

Today is:_____

The best part of my day was:

_____

_____

_____

_____

Something nice I did for someone today was:

_____

_____

_____

_____

Tonight I will pray for:

Because:

_____

_____

_____

_____

More about my day:

_____

_____

_____

_____

_____

Today is:_____

The best part of my day was:

_____

_____

_____

_____

Something nice I did for someone today was:

_____

_____

_____

_____

Tonight I will pray for:

Because:

_____

_____

_____

_____

More about my day:

_____

_____

_____

_____

Today is:_____

The best part of my day was:

_____
_____
_____
_____

Something nice I did for someone today was:

_____
_____
_____
_____

Tonight I will pray for:
Because:

_____
_____
_____
_____

More about my day:

_____
_____
_____
_____
_____

Today is:_____

The best part of my day was:

_____

_____

_____

_____

Something nice I did for someone today was:

_____

_____

_____

_____

Tonight I will pray for:

Because:

_____

_____

_____

_____

More about my day:

_____

_____

_____

_____

Today is:_____

The best part of my day was:

_____

_____

_____

_____

Something nice I did for someone today was:

_____

_____

_____

_____

Tonight I will pray for:

Because:

_____

_____

_____

_____

More about my day:

_____

_____

_____

_____

Today is:_____

The best part of my day was:

_____

_____

_____

_____

Something nice I did for someone today was:

_____

_____

_____

_____

Tonight I will pray for:

Because:

_____

_____

_____

_____

More about my day:

_____

_____

_____

_____

_____

Today is:_____

The best part of my day was:

_____

_____

_____

_____

Something nice I did for someone today was:

_____

_____

_____

_____

Tonight I will pray for:

Because:

_____

_____

_____

_____

More about my day:

_____

_____

_____

_____

_____

Today is:_____

The best part of my day was:

_____

_____

_____

_____

Something nice I did for someone today was:

_____

_____

_____

_____

Tonight I will pray for:

Because:

_____

_____

_____

_____

More about my day:

_____

_____

_____

_____

Today is:_____

The best part of my day was:

_____

_____

_____

_____

Something nice I did for someone today was:

_____

_____

_____

_____

Tonight I will pray for:

Because:

_____

_____

_____

_____

More about my day:

_____

_____

_____

_____

Today is:_____

The best part of my day was:

_____

_____

_____

_____

Something nice I did for someone today was:

_____

_____

_____

_____

Tonight I will pray for:

Because:

_____

_____

_____

_____

More about my day:

_____

_____

_____

_____

Today is:_____

The best part of my day was:

_____

_____

_____

_____

Something nice I did for someone today was:

_____

_____

_____

_____

Tonight I will pray for:

Because:

_____

_____

_____

_____

More about my day:

_____

_____

_____

_____

_____

Today is:_____

The best part of my day was:

_____

_____

_____

_____

Something nice I did for someone today was:

_____

_____

_____

_____

Tonight I will pray for:

Because:

_____

_____

_____

_____

More about my day:

_____

_____

_____

_____

_____

Today is:_____

The best part of my day was:

_____

_____

_____

_____

Something nice I did for someone today was:

_____

_____

_____

_____

Tonight I will pray for:
Because:

_____

_____

_____

_____

More about my day:

_____

_____

_____

_____

Today is:_____

The best part of my day was:

_____

_____

_____

_____

Something nice I did for someone today was:

_____

_____

_____

_____

Tonight I will pray for:

Because:

_____

_____

_____

_____

More about my day:

_____

_____

_____

_____

Today is:_____

The best part of my day was:

_____
_____
_____
_____

Something nice I did for someone today was:

_____
_____
_____
_____

Tonight I will pray for:

Because:

_____
_____
_____
_____

More about my day:

_____
_____
_____
_____
_____

Today is:_____

The best part of my day was:

_____

_____

_____

_____

Something nice I did for someone today was:

_____

_____

_____

_____

Tonight I will pray for:

Because:

_____

_____

_____

_____

More about my day:

_____

_____

_____

_____

Today is:_____

The best part of my day was:

_____

_____

_____

_____

Something nice I did for someone today was:

_____

_____

_____

_____

Tonight I will pray for:

Because:

_____

_____

_____

_____

More about my day:

_____

_____

_____

_____

Today is:_____

The best part of my day was:

_____

_____

_____

_____

Something nice I did for someone today was:

_____

_____

_____

_____

Tonight I will pray for:

Because:

_____

_____

_____

_____

More about my day:

_____

_____

_____

_____

Today is:_____

The best part of my day was:

_____

_____

_____

_____

Something nice I did for someone today was:

_____

_____

_____

_____

Tonight I will pray for:

Because:

_____

_____

_____

_____

More about my day:

_____

_____

_____

_____

_____

Today is:_____

The best part of my day was:

_____

_____

_____

_____

Something nice I did for someone today was:

_____

_____

_____

_____

Tonight I will pray for:

Because:

_____

_____

_____

_____

More about my day:

_____

_____

_____

_____

Today is:_____

The best part of my day was:

_____

_____

_____

_____

Something nice I did for someone today was:

_____

_____

_____

_____

Tonight I will pray for:

Because:

_____

_____

_____

_____

More about my day:

_____

_____

_____

_____

_____

Today is:_____

The best part of my day was:

_____

_____

_____

_____

Something nice I did for someone today was:

_____

_____

_____

_____

Tonight I will pray for:

Because:

_____

_____

_____

_____

More about my day:

_____

_____

_____

_____

Today is:_____

The best part of my day was:

_____

_____

_____

_____

Something nice I did for someone today was:

_____

_____

_____

_____

Tonight I will pray for:

Because:

_____

_____

_____

_____

More about my day:

_____

_____

_____

_____

Today is:_____

The best part of my day was:

_____

_____

_____

_____

Something nice I did for someone today was:

_____

_____

_____

_____

Tonight I will pray for:

Because:

_____

_____

_____

_____

More about my day:

_____

_____

_____

_____

Today is:_____

The best part of my day was:

_____

_____

_____

_____

Something nice I did for someone today was:

_____

_____

_____

_____

Tonight I will pray for:

Because:

_____

_____

_____

_____

More about my day:

_____

_____

_____

_____

_____

Today is:_____

The best part of my day was:

_____

_____

_____

_____

Something nice I did for someone today was:

_____

_____

_____

_____

Tonight I will pray for:

Because:

_____

_____

_____

_____

More about my day:

_____

_____

_____

_____

Today is:_____

The best part of my day was:

_____

_____

_____

_____

Something nice I did for someone today was:

_____

_____

_____

_____

Tonight I will pray for:
Because:

_____

_____

_____

_____

More about my day:

_____

_____

_____

_____

Today is:_____

The best part of my day was:

_____

_____

_____

_____

Something nice I did for someone today was:

_____

_____

_____

_____

Tonight I will pray for:

Because:

_____

_____

_____

_____

More about my day:

_____

_____

_____

_____

_____

Today is:_____

The best part of my day was:

_____

_____

_____

_____

Something nice I did for someone today was:

_____

_____

_____

_____

Tonight I will pray for:

Because:

_____

_____

_____

_____

More about my day:

_____

_____

_____

_____

_____

Today is:_____

The best part of my day was:

_____

_____

_____

_____

Something nice I did for someone today was:

_____

_____

_____

_____

Tonight I will pray for:

Because:

_____

_____

_____

_____

More about my day:

_____

_____

_____

_____

_____

Today is:_____

The best part of my day was:

_____

_____

_____

_____

Something nice I did for someone today was:

_____

_____

_____

_____

Tonight I will pray for:

Because:

_____

_____

_____

_____

More about my day:

_____

_____

_____

_____

_____

Today is:_____

The best part of my day was:

_____

_____

_____

_____

Something nice I did for someone today was:

_____

_____

_____

_____

Tonight I will pray for:

Because:

_____

_____

_____

_____

More about my day:

_____

_____

_____

_____

Today is:_____

The best part of my day was:

_____

_____

_____

_____

Something nice I did for someone today was:

_____

_____

_____

_____

Tonight I will pray for:

Because:

_____

_____

_____

_____

More about my day:

_____

_____

_____

_____

_____

Today is:_____

The best part of my day was:

_____

_____

_____

_____

Something nice I did for someone today was:

_____

_____

_____

_____

Tonight I will pray for:

Because:

_____

_____

_____

_____

More about my day:

_____

_____

_____

_____

Today is:_____

The best part of my day was:

_____

_____

_____

_____

Something nice I did for someone today was:

_____

_____

_____

_____

Tonight I will pray for:

Because:

_____

_____

_____

_____

More about my day:

_____

_____

_____

_____

Today is:_____

The best part of my day was:

_____
_____
_____
_____

Something nice I did for someone today was:

_____
_____
_____
_____

Tonight I will pray for:
Because:

_____
_____
_____
_____

More about my day:

_____
_____
_____
_____
_____

Today is:_____

The best part of my day was:

_____

_____

_____

_____

Something nice I did for someone today was:

_____

_____

_____

_____

Tonight I will pray for:

Because:

_____

_____

_____

_____

More about my day:

_____

_____

_____

_____

_____

Today is:_____

The best part of my day was:

_____

_____

_____

_____

Something nice I did for someone today was:

_____

_____

_____

_____

Tonight I will pray for:

Because:

_____

_____

_____

_____

More about my day:

_____

_____

_____

_____

Today is:_____

The best part of my day was:

_____

_____

_____

_____

Something nice I did for someone today was:

_____

_____

_____

_____

Tonight I will pray for:

Because:

_____

_____

_____

_____

More about my day:

_____

_____

_____

_____

_____

Today is:_____

The best part of my day was:

_____

_____

_____

_____

Something nice I did for someone today was:

_____

_____

_____

_____

Tonight I will pray for:

Because:

_____

_____

_____

_____

More about my day:

_____

_____

_____

_____

Today is:_____

The best part of my day was:

_____

_____

_____

_____

Something nice I did for someone today was:

_____

_____

_____

_____

Tonight I will pray for:

Because:

_____

_____

_____

_____

More about my day:

_____

_____

_____

_____

_____

Today is:_____

The best part of my day was:

_____

_____

_____

_____

Something nice I did for someone today was:

_____

_____

_____

_____

Tonight I will pray for:

Because:

_____

_____

_____

_____

More about my day:

_____

_____

_____

_____

Today is:_____

The best part of my day was:

_____

_____

_____

_____

Something nice I did for someone today was:

_____

_____

_____

_____

Tonight I will pray for:

Because:

_____

_____

_____

_____

More about my day:

_____

_____

_____

_____

Today is:_____

The best part of my day was:

_____

_____

_____

_____

Something nice I did for someone today was:

_____

_____

_____

_____

Tonight I will pray for:

Because:

_____

_____

_____

_____

More about my day:

_____

_____

_____

_____

Today is:_____

The best part of my day was:

_____

_____

_____

_____

Something nice I did for someone today was:

_____

_____

_____

Tonight I will pray for:

Because:

_____

_____

_____

_____

More about my day:

_____

_____

_____

_____

Today is:_____

The best part of my day was:

_____

_____

_____

_____

Something nice I did for someone today was:

_____

_____

_____

_____

Tonight I will pray for:

Because:

_____

_____

_____

_____

More about my day:

_____

_____

_____

_____

_____

Today is:_____

The best part of my day was:

_____

_____

_____

_____

Something nice I did for someone today was:

_____

_____

_____

Tonight I will pray for:

Because:

_____

_____

_____

_____

More about my day:

_____

_____

_____

_____

_____

Today is:_____

The best part of my day was:

_____

_____

_____

_____

Something nice I did for someone today was:

_____

_____

_____

_____

Tonight I will pray for:

Because:

_____

_____

_____

_____

More about my day:

_____

_____

_____

_____

Today is:_____

The best part of my day was:

_____

_____

_____

_____

Something nice I did for someone today was:

_____

_____

_____

_____

Tonight I will pray for:

Because:

_____

_____

_____

_____

More about my day:

_____

_____

_____

_____

_____

Today is:_____

The best part of my day was:

_____

_____

_____

_____

Something nice I did for someone today was:

_____

_____

_____

_____

Tonight I will pray for:

Because:

_____

_____

_____

_____

More about my day:

_____

_____

_____

_____

Today is:_____

The best part of my day was:

_____
_____
_____
_____

Something nice I did for someone today was:

_____
_____
_____
_____

Tonight I will pray for:
Because:

_____
_____
_____
_____

More about my day:

_____
_____
_____
_____
_____

Today is:_____

The best part of my day was:

_____

_____

_____

_____

Something nice I did for someone today was:

_____

_____

_____

_____

Tonight I will pray for:

Because:

_____

_____

_____

_____

More about my day:

_____

_____

_____

_____

Today is:_____

The best part of my day was:

_____

_____

_____

_____

Something nice I did for someone today was:

_____

_____

_____

_____

Tonight I will pray for:

Because:

_____

_____

_____

_____

More about my day:

_____

_____

_____

_____

Today is:_____

The best part of my day was:

_____

_____

_____

_____

Something nice I did for someone today was:

_____

_____

_____

_____

Tonight I will pray for:

Because:

_____

_____

_____

_____

More about my day:

_____

_____

_____

_____

Today is:_____

The best part of my day was:

_____

_____

_____

_____

Something nice I did for someone today was:

_____

_____

_____

_____

Tonight I will pray for:

Because:

_____

_____

_____

_____

More about my day:

_____

_____

_____

_____

Today is:_____

The best part of my day was:

_____

_____

_____

_____

Something nice I did for someone today was:

_____

_____

_____

_____

Tonight I will pray for:

Because:

_____

_____

_____

_____

More about my day:

_____

_____

_____

_____

Today is:_____

The best part of my day was:

_____

_____

_____

_____

Something nice I did for someone today was:

_____

_____

_____

_____

Tonight I will pray for:

Because:

_____

_____

_____

_____

More about my day:

_____

_____

_____

_____

Today is:_____

The best part of my day was:

_____

_____

_____

_____

Something nice I did for someone today was:

_____

_____

_____

_____

Tonight I will pray for:

Because:

_____

_____

_____

_____

More about my day:

_____

_____

_____

_____

Today is:_____

The best part of my day was:

_____

_____

_____

_____

Something nice I did for someone today was:

_____

_____

_____

_____

Tonight I will pray for:

Because:

_____

_____

_____

_____

More about my day:

_____

_____

_____

_____

_____

Today is:_____

The best part of my day was:

_____

_____

_____

_____

Something nice I did for someone today was:

_____

_____

_____

_____

Tonight I will pray for:

Because:

_____

_____

_____

_____

More about my day:

_____

_____

_____

_____

Today is:_____

The best part of my day was:

_____

_____

_____

_____

Something nice I did for someone today was:

_____

_____

_____

_____

Tonight I will pray for:
Because:

_____

_____

_____

_____

More about my day:

_____

_____

_____

_____

_____

Today is:_____

The best part of my day was:

_____
_____
_____
_____

Something nice I did for someone today was:

_____
_____
_____
_____

Tonight I will pray for:

Because:

_____
_____
_____
_____

More about my day:

_____
_____
_____
_____

Today is:_____

The best part of my day was:

_____

_____

_____

_____

Something nice I did for someone today was:

_____

_____

_____

Tonight I will pray for:

Because:

_____

_____

_____

_____

More about my day:

_____

_____

_____

_____

_____

Today is:_____

The best part of my day was:

_____

_____

_____

_____

Something nice I did for someone today was:

_____

_____

_____

_____

Tonight I will pray for:

Because:

_____

_____

_____

_____

More about my day:

_____

_____

_____

_____

Today is:_____

The best part of my day was:

_____

_____

_____

_____

Something nice I did for someone today was:

_____

_____

_____

Tonight I will pray for:

Because:

_____

_____

_____

_____

More about my day:

_____

_____

_____

_____

Today is:_____

The best part of my day was:

_____

_____

_____

_____

Something nice I did for someone today was:

_____

_____

_____

_____

Tonight I will pray for:

Because:

_____

_____

_____

_____

More about my day:

_____

_____

_____

_____

Today is:_____

The best part of my day was:

_____

_____

_____

_____

Something nice I did for someone today was:

_____

_____

_____

_____

Tonight I will pray for:
Because:

_____

_____

_____

_____

More about my day:

_____

_____

_____

_____

_____

Today is:_____

The best part of my day was:

_____

_____

_____

_____

Something nice I did for someone today was:

_____

_____

_____

_____

Tonight I will pray for:

Because:

_____

_____

_____

_____

More about my day:

_____

_____

_____

_____

_____

Today is:_____

The best part of my day was:

_____

_____

_____

_____

Something nice I did for someone today was:

_____

_____

_____

Tonight I will pray for:

Because:

_____

_____

_____

_____

More about my day:

_____

_____

_____

_____

Today is:_____

The best part of my day was:

_____

_____

_____

_____

Something nice I did for someone today was:

_____

_____

_____

_____

Tonight I will pray for:

Because:

_____

_____

_____

_____

More about my day:

_____

_____

_____

_____

Today is:_____

The best part of my day was:

_____

_____

_____

_____

Something nice I did for someone today was:

_____

_____

_____

_____

Tonight I will pray for:

Because:

_____

_____

_____

_____

More about my day:

_____

_____

_____

_____

_____

Today is:_____

The best part of my day was:

_____

_____

_____

_____

Something nice I did for someone today was:

_____

_____

_____

_____

Tonight I will pray for:

Because:

_____

_____

_____

_____

More about my day:

_____

_____

_____

_____

_____

Today is:_____

The best part of my day was:

_____

_____

_____

_____

Something nice I did for someone today was:

_____

_____

_____

_____

Tonight I will pray for:

Because:

_____

_____

_____

_____

More about my day:

_____

_____

_____

_____

_____

Today is:_____

The best part of my day was:

_____

_____

_____

_____

Something nice I did for someone today was:

_____

_____

_____

_____

Tonight I will pray for:

Because:

_____

_____

_____

_____

More about my day:

_____

_____

_____

_____

Today is:_____

The best part of my day was:

_____

_____

_____

_____

Something nice I did for someone today was:

_____

_____

_____

Tonight I will pray for:

Because:

_____

_____

_____

_____

More about my day:

_____

_____

_____

_____

_____

Today is:_____

The best part of my day was:

_____

_____

_____

_____

Something nice I did for someone today was:

_____

_____

_____

_____

Tonight I will pray for:

Because:

_____

_____

_____

_____

More about my day:

_____

_____

_____

_____

Today is:_____

The best part of my day was:

_____

_____

_____

_____

Something nice I did for someone today was:

_____

_____

_____

_____

Tonight I will pray for:

Because:

_____

_____

_____

_____

More about my day:

_____

_____

_____

_____

_____

Today is:_____

The best part of my day was:

_____

_____

_____

_____

Something nice I did for someone today was:

_____

_____

_____

_____

Tonight I will pray for:

Because:

_____

_____

_____

_____

More about my day:

_____

_____

_____

_____

Today is:_____

The best part of my day was:

_____

_____

_____

_____

Something nice I did for someone today was:

_____

_____

_____

_____

Tonight I will pray for:

Because:

_____

_____

_____

_____

More about my day:

_____

_____

_____

_____

Today is:_____

The best part of my day was:

_____

_____

_____

_____

Something nice I did for someone today was:

_____

_____

_____

_____

Tonight I will pray for:

Because:

_____

_____

_____

_____

More about my day:

_____

_____

_____

_____

Today is:_____

The best part of my day was:

_____

_____

_____

_____

Something nice I did for someone today was:

_____

_____

_____

_____

Tonight I will pray for:

Because:

_____

_____

_____

_____

More about my day:

_____

_____

_____

_____

_____

Today is:_____

The best part of my day was:

_____

_____

_____

_____

Something nice I did for someone today was:

_____

_____

_____

_____

Tonight I will pray for:

Because:

_____

_____

_____

_____

More about my day:

_____

_____

_____

_____

Today is:_____

The best part of my day was:

_____

_____

_____

_____

Something nice I did for someone today was:

_____

_____

_____

_____

Tonight I will pray for:

Because:

_____

_____

_____

_____

More about my day:

_____

_____

_____

_____

_____

Today is:_____

The best part of my day was:

_____

_____

_____

_____

Something nice I did for someone today was:

_____

_____

_____

_____

Tonight I will pray for:

Because:

_____

_____

_____

_____

More about my day:

_____

_____

_____

_____

Today is:_____

The best part of my day was:

_____

_____

_____

_____

Something nice I did for someone today was:

_____

_____

_____

_____

Tonight I will pray for:

Because:

_____

_____

_____

_____

More about my day:

_____

_____

_____

_____

_____

Today is:_____

The best part of my day was:

_____

_____

_____

_____

Something nice I did for someone today was:

_____

_____

_____

_____

Tonight I will pray for:

Because:

_____

_____

_____

_____

More about my day:

_____

_____

_____

_____

Today is:_____

The best part of my day was:

_____

_____

_____

_____

Something nice I did for someone today was:

_____

_____

_____

_____

Tonight I will pray for:

Because:

_____

_____

_____

_____

More about my day:

_____

_____

_____

_____

Today is:_____

The best part of my day was:

_____

_____

_____

_____

Something nice I did for someone today was:

_____

_____

_____

_____

Tonight I will pray for:

Because:

_____

_____

_____

_____

More about my day:

_____

_____

_____

_____

Today is:_____

The best part of my day was:

_____

_____

_____

_____

Something nice I did for someone today was:

_____

_____

_____

_____

Tonight I will pray for:

Because:

_____

_____

_____

_____

More about my day:

_____

_____

_____

_____

_____

Today is:_____

The best part of my day was:

_____

_____

_____

_____

Something nice I did for someone today was:

_____

_____

_____

_____

Tonight I will pray for:

Because:

_____

_____

_____

_____

More about my day:

_____

_____

_____

_____

Today is:_____

The best part of my day was:

_____

_____

_____

_____

Something nice I did for someone today was:

_____

_____

_____

_____

Tonight I will pray for:

Because:

_____

_____

_____

_____

More about my day:

_____

_____

_____

_____

_____

Today is:_____

The best part of my day was:

_____

_____

_____

_____

Something nice I did for someone today was:

_____

_____

_____

_____

Tonight I will pray for:

Because:

_____

_____

_____

_____

More about my day:

_____

_____

_____

_____

Today is:_____

The best part of my day was:

_____

_____

_____

_____

Something nice I did for someone today was:

_____

_____

_____

_____

Tonight I will pray for:

Because:

_____

_____

_____

_____

More about my day:

_____

_____

_____

_____

Today is:_____

The best part of my day was:

_____

_____

_____

_____

Something nice I did for someone today was:

_____

_____

_____

_____

Tonight I will pray for:
Because:

_____

_____

_____

_____

More about my day:

_____

_____

_____

_____

_____

Today is:_____

The best part of my day was:

_____

_____

_____

_____

Something nice I did for someone today was:

_____

_____

_____

_____

Tonight I will pray for:

Because:

_____

_____

_____

_____

More about my day:

_____

_____

_____

_____

Today is:_____

The best part of my day was:

_____

_____

_____

_____

Something nice I did for someone today was:

_____

_____

_____

_____

Tonight I will pray for:

Because:

_____

_____

_____

_____

More about my day:

_____

_____

_____

_____

Today is:_____

The best part of my day was:

_____

_____

_____

_____

Something nice I did for someone today was:

_____

_____

_____

_____

Tonight I will pray for:

Because:

_____

_____

_____

_____

More about my day:

_____

_____

_____

_____

_____

Today is:_____

The best part of my day was:

_____

_____

_____

_____

Something nice I did for someone today was:

_____

_____

_____

_____

Tonight I will pray for:

Because:

_____

_____

_____

_____

More about my day:

_____

_____

_____

_____

Today is:_____

The best part of my day was:

_____

_____

_____

_____

Something nice I did for someone today was:

_____

_____

_____

_____

Tonight I will pray for:

Because:

_____

_____

_____

_____

More about my day:

_____

_____

_____

_____

Today is:_____

The best part of my day was:

_____

_____

_____

_____

Something nice I did for someone today was:

_____

_____

_____

_____

Tonight I will pray for:

Because:

_____

_____

_____

_____

More about my day:

_____

_____

_____

_____

Today is:_____

The best part of my day was:

_____

_____

_____

_____

Something nice I did for someone today was:

_____

_____

_____

_____

Tonight I will pray for:

Because:

_____

_____

_____

_____

More about my day:

_____

_____

_____

_____

_____

Today is:_____

The best part of my day was:

_____

_____

_____

_____

Something nice I did for someone today was:

_____

_____

_____

_____

Tonight I will pray for:

Because:

_____

_____

_____

_____

More about my day:

_____

_____

_____

_____

_____

Today is:_____

The best part of my day was:

_____

_____

_____

_____

Something nice I did for someone today was:

_____

_____

_____

_____

Tonight I will pray for:

Because:

_____

_____

_____

_____

More about my day:

_____

_____

_____

_____

_____

Today is:_____

The best part of my day was:

_____

_____

_____

_____

Something nice I did for someone today was:

_____

_____

_____

_____

Tonight I will pray for:

Because:

_____

_____

_____

_____

More about my day:

_____

_____

_____

_____

Today is:_____

The best part of my day was:

_____

_____

_____

_____

Something nice I did for someone today was:

_____

_____

_____

_____

Tonight I will pray for:

Because:

_____

_____

_____

_____

More about my day:

_____

_____

_____

_____

_____

Today is:_____

The best part of my day was:

_____

_____

_____

Something nice I did for someone today was:

_____

_____

_____

Tonight I will pray for:
Because:

_____

_____

_____

More about my day:

_____

_____

_____

_____

Today is:_____

The best part of my day was:

_____

_____

_____

_____

Something nice I did for someone today was:

_____

_____

_____

_____

Tonight I will pray for:

Because:

_____

_____

_____

_____

More about my day:

_____

_____

_____

_____

_____

Today is:_____

The best part of my day was:

_____

_____

_____

_____

Something nice I did for someone today was:

_____

_____

_____

_____

Tonight I will pray for:
Because:

_____

_____

_____

_____

More about my day:

_____

_____

_____

_____

Today is:_____

The best part of my day was:

_____

_____

_____

_____

Something nice I did for someone today was:

_____

_____

_____

_____

Tonight I will pray for:

Because:

_____

_____

_____

_____

More about my day:

_____

_____

_____

_____

_____

Today is:_____

The best part of my day was:

_____

_____

_____

Something nice I did for someone today was:

_____

_____

_____

Tonight I will pray for:

Because:

_____

_____

_____

More about my day:

_____

_____

_____

_____

Today is:_____

The best part of my day was:

_____

_____

_____

_____

Something nice I did for someone today was:

_____

_____

_____

_____

Tonight I will pray for:

Because:

_____

_____

_____

_____

More about my day:

_____

_____

_____

_____

Today is:_____

The best part of my day was:

_____

_____

_____

_____

Something nice I did for someone today was:

_____

_____

_____

_____

Tonight I will pray for:

Because:

_____

_____

_____

_____

More about my day:

_____

_____

_____

_____

Today is:_____

The best part of my day was:

_____

_____

_____

_____

Something nice I did for someone today was:

_____

_____

_____

_____

Tonight I will pray for:

Because:

_____

_____

_____

_____

More about my day:

_____

_____

_____

_____

_____

Today is:_____

The best part of my day was:

_____
_____
_____
_____

Something nice I did for someone today was:

_____
_____
_____
_____

Tonight I will pray for:
Because:

_____
_____
_____
_____

More about my day:

_____
_____
_____
_____

Today is:_____

The best part of my day was:

_____

_____

_____

_____

Something nice I did for someone today was:

_____

_____

_____

_____

Tonight I will pray for:

Because:

_____

_____

_____

_____

More about my day:

_____

_____

_____

_____

_____

Today is:_____

The best part of my day was:

_____

_____

_____

_____

Something nice I did for someone today was:

_____

_____

_____

_____

Tonight I will pray for:

Because:

_____

_____

_____

_____

More about my day:

_____

_____

_____

_____

Today is:_____

The best part of my day was:

_____

_____

_____

_____

Something nice I did for someone today was:

_____

_____

_____

_____

Tonight I will pray for:

Because:

_____

_____

_____

_____

More about my day:

_____

_____

_____

_____

_____

Today is:_____

The best part of my day was:

_____

_____

_____

_____

Something nice I did for someone today was:

_____

_____

_____

_____

Tonight I will pray for:

Because:

_____

_____

_____

_____

More about my day:

_____

_____

_____

_____

Today is:_____

The best part of my day was:

_____

_____

_____

_____

Something nice I did for someone today was:

_____

_____

_____

_____

Tonight I will pray for:

Because:

_____

_____

_____

_____

More about my day:

_____

_____

_____

_____

_____

Today is:_____

The best part of my day was:

_____

_____

_____

_____

Something nice I did for someone today was:

_____

_____

_____

_____

Tonight I will pray for:

Because:

_____

_____

_____

_____

More about my day:

_____

_____

_____

_____

Today is:_____

The best part of my day was:

_____

_____

_____

_____

Something nice I did for someone today was:

_____

_____

_____

_____

Tonight I will pray for:

Because:

_____

_____

_____

_____

More about my day:

_____

_____

_____

_____

_____

Today is:_____

The best part of my day was:

_____

_____

_____

_____

Something nice I did for someone today was:

_____

_____

_____

_____

Tonight I will pray for:

Because:

_____

_____

_____

_____

More about my day:

_____

_____

_____

_____

_____

Today is:_____

The best part of my day was:

_____

_____

_____

_____

Something nice I did for someone today was:

_____

_____

_____

_____

Tonight I will pray for:

Because:

_____

_____

_____

_____

More about my day:

_____

_____

_____

_____

_____

Today is:_____

The best part of my day was:

_____

_____

_____

_____

Something nice I did for someone today was:

_____

_____

_____

_____

Tonight I will pray for:

Because:

_____

_____

_____

_____

More about my day:

_____

_____

_____

_____

Today is:_____

The best part of my day was:

_____

_____

_____

_____

Something nice I did for someone today was:

_____

_____

_____

_____

Tonight I will pray for:

Because:

_____

_____

_____

_____

More about my day:

_____

_____

_____

_____

Today is:_____

The best part of my day was:

_____

_____

_____

_____

Something nice I did for someone today was:

_____

_____

_____

_____

Tonight I will pray for:

Because:

_____

_____

_____

_____

More about my day:

_____

_____

_____

_____

Today is:_____

The best part of my day was:

_____

_____

_____

_____

Something nice I did for someone today was:

_____

_____

_____

_____

Tonight I will pray for:

Because:

_____

_____

_____

_____

More about my day:

_____

_____

_____

_____

Today is:_____

The best part of my day was:

_____

_____

_____

_____

Something nice I did for someone today was:

_____

_____

_____

_____

Tonight I will pray for:

Because:

_____

_____

_____

_____

More about my day:

_____

_____

_____

_____

Today is:_____

The best part of my day was:

_____

_____

_____

_____

Something nice I did for someone today was:

_____

_____

_____

_____

Tonight I will pray for:

Because:

_____

_____

_____

_____

More about my day:

_____

_____

_____

_____

Today is:_____

The best part of my day was:

_____

_____

_____

_____

Something nice I did for someone today was:

_____

_____

_____

_____

Tonight I will pray for:

Because:

_____

_____

_____

_____

More about my day:

_____

_____

_____

_____

_____

Today is:_____

The best part of my day was:

_____

_____

_____

_____

Something nice I did for someone today was:

_____

_____

_____

_____

Tonight I will pray for:

Because:

_____

_____

_____

_____

More about my day:

_____

_____

_____

_____

_____

Today is:_____

The best part of my day was:

_____

_____

_____

_____

Something nice I did for someone today was:

_____

_____

_____

_____

Tonight I will pray for:

Because:

_____

_____

_____

_____

More about my day:

_____

_____

_____

_____

_____

Today is:_____

The best part of my day was:

_____

_____

_____

_____

Something nice I did for someone today was:

_____

_____

_____

_____

Tonight I will pray for:

Because:

_____

_____

_____

_____

More about my day:

_____

_____

_____

_____

_____

Today is:_____

The best part of my day was:

_____

_____

_____

_____

Something nice I did for someone today was:

_____

_____

_____

_____

Tonight I will pray for:

Because:

_____

_____

_____

_____

More about my day:

_____

_____

_____

_____

Today is:_____

The best part of my day was:

_____

_____

_____

_____

Something nice I did for someone today was:

_____

_____

_____

_____

Tonight I will pray for:

Because:

_____

_____

_____

_____

More about my day:

_____

_____

_____

_____

_____

Today is:_____

The best part of my day was:

_____

_____

_____

_____

Something nice I did for someone today was:

_____

_____

_____

_____

Tonight I will pray for:

Because:

_____

_____

_____

_____

More about my day:

_____

_____

_____

_____

Today is:_____

The best part of my day was:

_____

_____

_____

_____

Something nice I did for someone today was:

_____

_____

_____

_____

Tonight I will pray for:
Because:

_____

_____

_____

_____

More about my day:

_____

_____

_____

_____

Today is:_____

The best part of my day was:

_____

_____

_____

_____

Something nice I did for someone today was:

_____

_____

_____

_____

Tonight I will pray for:
Because:

_____

_____

_____

_____

More about my day:

_____

_____

_____

_____

Today is:_____

The best part of my day was:

_____

_____

_____

_____

Something nice I did for someone today was:

_____

_____

_____

_____

Tonight I will pray for:

Because:

_____

_____

_____

_____

More about my day:

_____

_____

_____

_____

_____

Today is:_____

The best part of my day was:

_____

_____

_____

_____

Something nice I did for someone today was:

_____

_____

_____

_____

Tonight I will pray for:

Because:

_____

_____

_____

_____

More about my day:

_____

_____

_____

_____

Today is:_____

The best part of my day was:

_____

_____

_____

_____

Something nice I did for someone today was:

_____

_____

_____

_____

Tonight I will pray for:

Because:

_____

_____

_____

_____

More about my day:

_____

_____

_____

_____

Today is:_____

The best part of my day was:

_____

_____

_____

_____

Something nice I did for someone today was:

_____

_____

_____

_____

Tonight I will pray for:

Because:

_____

_____

_____

_____

More about my day:

_____

_____

_____

_____

_____

Today is:_____

The best part of my day was:

_____

_____

_____

_____

Something nice I did for someone today was:

_____

_____

_____

_____

Tonight I will pray for:

Because:

_____

_____

_____

_____

More about my day:

_____

_____

_____

_____

_____

Today is:_____

The best part of my day was:

_____

_____

_____

_____

Something nice I did for someone today was:

_____

_____

_____

_____

Tonight I will pray for:

Because:

_____

_____

_____

_____

More about my day:

_____

_____

_____

_____

_____

Today is:_____

The best part of my day was:

_____

_____

_____

_____

Something nice I did for someone today was:

_____

_____

_____

_____

Tonight I will pray for:

Because:

_____

_____

_____

_____

More about my day:

_____

_____

_____

_____

_____

Today is:_____

The best part of my day was:

_____

_____

_____

_____

Something nice I did for someone today was:

_____

_____

_____

_____

Tonight I will pray for:

Because:

_____

_____

_____

_____

More about my day:

_____

_____

_____

_____

_____

Today is:_____

The best part of my day was:

_____

_____

_____

_____

Something nice I did for someone today was:

_____

_____

_____

_____

Tonight I will pray for:

Because:

_____

_____

_____

_____

More about my day:

_____

_____

_____

_____

Today is:_____

The best part of my day was:

_____

_____

_____

_____

Something nice I did for someone today was:

_____

_____

_____

_____

Tonight I will pray for:
Because:

_____

_____

_____

_____

More about my day:

_____

_____

_____

_____

Today is:_____

The best part of my day was:

_____

_____

_____

_____

Something nice I did for someone today was:

_____

_____

_____

_____

Tonight I will pray for:

Because:

_____

_____

_____

_____

More about my day:

_____

_____

_____

_____

_____

Today is:_____

The best part of my day was:

_____

_____

_____

_____

Something nice I did for someone today was:

_____

_____

_____

_____

Tonight I will pray for:

Because:

_____

_____

_____

_____

More about my day:

_____

_____

_____

_____

_____

Today is:_____

The best part of my day was:

_____

_____

_____

_____

Something nice I did for someone today was:

_____

_____

_____

_____

Tonight I will pray for:

Because:

_____

_____

_____

_____

More about my day:

_____

_____

_____

_____

Today is:_____

The best part of my day was:

_____

_____

_____

_____

Something nice I did for someone today was:

_____

_____

_____

_____

Tonight I will pray for:
Because:

_____

_____

_____

_____

More about my day:

_____

_____

_____

_____

Today is:_____

The best part of my day was:

_____

_____

_____

_____

Something nice I did for someone today was:

_____

_____

_____

_____

Tonight I will pray for:
Because:

_____

_____

_____

_____

More about my day:

_____

_____

_____

_____

Today is:_____

The best part of my day was:

_____

_____

_____

_____

Something nice I did for someone today was:

_____

_____

_____

_____

Tonight I will pray for:

Because:

_____

_____

_____

_____

More about my day:

_____

_____

_____

_____

Today is:_____

The best part of my day was:

_____

_____

_____

_____

Something nice I did for someone today was:

_____

_____

_____

_____

Tonight I will pray for:
Because:

_____

_____

_____

_____

More about my day:

_____

_____

_____

_____

Today is:_____

The best part of my day was:

_____

_____

_____

_____

Something nice I did for someone today was:

_____

_____

_____

_____

Tonight I will pray for:

Because:

_____

_____

_____

_____

More about my day:

_____

_____

_____

_____

Today is:_____

The best part of my day was:

_____
_____
_____
_____

Something nice I did for someone today was:

_____
_____
_____
_____

Tonight I will pray for:

Because:

_____
_____
_____
_____

More about my day:

_____
_____
_____
_____
_____

Today is:_____

The best part of my day was:

_____

_____

_____

_____

Something nice I did for someone today was:

_____

_____

_____

_____

Tonight I will pray for:
Because:

_____

_____

_____

_____

More about my day:

_____

_____

_____

_____

_____

Today is:_____

The best part of my day was:

_____
_____
_____
_____

Something nice I did for someone today was:

_____
_____
_____
_____

Tonight I will pray for:
Because:

_____
_____
_____
_____

More about my day:

_____
_____
_____
_____

Today is:_____

The best part of my day was:

_____

_____

_____

_____

Something nice I did for someone today was:

_____

_____

_____

_____

Tonight I will pray for:

Because:

_____

_____

_____

_____

More about my day:

_____

_____

_____

_____

Today is:_____

The best part of my day was:

_____

_____

_____

_____

Something nice I did for someone today was:

_____

_____

_____

_____

Tonight I will pray for:

Because:

_____

_____

_____

_____

More about my day:

_____

_____

_____

_____

_____

Today is:_____

The best part of my day was:

_____

_____

_____

_____

Something nice I did for someone today was:

_____

_____

_____

_____

Tonight I will pray for:

Because:

_____

_____

_____

_____

More about my day:

_____

_____

_____

_____

_____

Today is:_____

The best part of my day was:

_____

_____

_____

_____

Something nice I did for someone today was:

_____

_____

_____

_____

Tonight I will pray for:

Because:

_____

_____

_____

_____

More about my day:

_____

_____

_____

_____

Today is:_____

The best part of my day was:

_____

_____

_____

_____

Something nice I did for someone today was:

_____

_____

_____

_____

Tonight I will pray for:

Because:

_____

_____

_____

_____

More about my day:

_____

_____

_____

_____

Today is:_____

The best part of my day was:

_____

_____

_____

_____

Something nice I did for someone today was:

_____

_____

_____

_____

Tonight I will pray for:

Because:

_____

_____

_____

_____

More about my day:

_____

_____

_____

_____

_____

Today is:_____

The best part of my day was:

_____

_____

_____

_____

Something nice I did for someone today was:

_____

_____

_____

_____

Tonight I will pray for:

Because:

_____

_____

_____

_____

More about my day:

_____

_____

_____

_____

_____

Today is:_____

The best part of my day was:

_____

_____

_____

_____

Something nice I did for someone today was:

_____

_____

_____

_____

Tonight I will pray for:
Because:

_____

_____

_____

_____

More about my day:

_____

_____

_____

_____

Today is:_____

The best part of my day was:

_____

_____

_____

_____

Something nice I did for someone today was:

_____

_____

_____

_____

Tonight I will pray for:

Because:

_____

_____

_____

_____

More about my day:

_____

_____

_____

_____

_____

Today is:_____

The best part of my day was:

_____

_____

_____

_____

Something nice I did for someone today was:

_____

_____

_____

_____

Tonight I will pray for:

Because:

_____

_____

_____

_____

More about my day:

_____

_____

_____

_____

Today is:_____

The best part of my day was:

_____

_____

_____

_____

Something nice I did for someone today was:

_____

_____

_____

_____

Tonight I will pray for:
Because:

_____

_____

_____

_____

More about my day:

_____

_____

_____

_____

_____

Today is:_____

The best part of my day was:

_____

_____

_____

_____

Something nice I did for someone today was:

_____

_____

_____

_____

Tonight I will pray for:

Because:

_____

_____

_____

_____

More about my day:

_____

_____

_____

_____

Today is:_____

The best part of my day was:

_____

_____

_____

Something nice I did for someone today was:

_____

_____

_____

Tonight I will pray for:

Because:

_____

_____

_____

More about my day:

_____

_____

_____

_____

Today is:_____

The best part of my day was:

_____

_____

_____

_____

Something nice I did for someone today was:

_____

_____

_____

_____

Tonight I will pray for:

Because:

_____

_____

_____

_____

More about my day:

_____

_____

_____

_____

Today is:_____

The best part of my day was:

_____

_____

_____

_____

Something nice I did for someone today was:

_____

_____

_____

_____

Tonight I will pray for:

Because:

_____

_____

_____

_____

More about my day:

_____

_____

_____

_____

_____

Today is:_____

The best part of my day was:

_____

_____

_____

_____

Something nice I did for someone today was:

_____

_____

_____

_____

Tonight I will pray for:

Because:

_____

_____

_____

_____

More about my day:

_____

_____

_____

_____

_____

Today is:_____

The best part of my day was:

_____

_____

_____

_____

Something nice I did for someone today was:

_____

_____

_____

_____

Tonight I will pray for:
Because:

_____

_____

_____

_____

More about my day:

_____

_____

_____

_____

_____

Today is:_____

The best part of my day was:

_____

_____

_____

_____

Something nice I did for someone today was:

_____

_____

_____

_____

Tonight I will pray for:

Because:

_____

_____

_____

_____

More about my day:

_____

_____

_____

_____

Today is:_____

The best part of my day was:

_____

_____

_____

_____

Something nice I did for someone today was:

_____

_____

_____

_____

Tonight I will pray for:
Because:

_____

_____

_____

_____

More about my day:

_____

_____

_____

_____

_____

Today is:_____

The best part of my day was:

_____

_____

_____

_____

Something nice I did for someone today was:

_____

_____

_____

_____

Tonight I will pray for:

Because:

_____

_____

_____

_____

More about my day:

_____

_____

_____

_____

Today is:_____

The best part of my day was:

_____

_____

_____

_____

Something nice I did for someone today was:

_____

_____

_____

_____

Tonight I will pray for:

Because:

_____

_____

_____

_____

More about my day:

_____

_____

_____

_____

_____

Today is:_____

The best part of my day was:

_____

_____

_____

_____

Something nice I did for someone today was:

_____

_____

_____

_____

Tonight I will pray for:

Because:

_____

_____

_____

_____

More about my day:

_____

_____

_____

_____

Today is:_____

The best part of my day was:

_____

_____

_____

_____

Something nice I did for someone today was:

_____

_____

_____

_____

Tonight I will pray for:

Because:

_____

_____

_____

_____

More about my day:

_____

_____

_____

_____

Today is:_____

The best part of my day was:

_____

_____

_____

_____

Something nice I did for someone today was:

_____

_____

_____

_____

Tonight I will pray for:

Because:

_____

_____

_____

_____

More about my day:

_____

_____

_____

_____

Today is:_____

The best part of my day was:

_____

_____

_____

_____

Something nice I did for someone today was:

_____

_____

_____

_____

Tonight I will pray for:

Because:

_____

_____

_____

_____

More about my day:

_____

_____

_____

_____

_____

Today is:_____

The best part of my day was:

_____

_____

_____

_____

Something nice I did for someone today was:

_____

_____

_____

_____

Tonight I will pray for:

Because:

_____

_____

_____

_____

More about my day:

_____

_____

_____

_____

Today is:_____

The best part of my day was:

_____

_____

_____

_____

Something nice I did for someone today was:

_____

_____

_____

_____

Tonight I will pray for:

Because:

_____

_____

_____

_____

More about my day:

_____

_____

_____

_____

_____

Today is:_____

The best part of my day was:

_____

_____

_____

_____

Something nice I did for someone today was:

_____

_____

_____

_____

Tonight I will pray for:

Because:

_____

_____

_____

_____

More about my day:

_____

_____

_____

_____

Today is:_____

The best part of my day was:

_____
_____
_____
_____

Something nice I did for someone today was:

_____
_____
_____
_____

Tonight I will pray for:

Because:

_____
_____
_____
_____

More about my day:

_____
_____
_____
_____
_____

Today is:_____

The best part of my day was:

_____

_____

_____

_____

Something nice I did for someone today was:

_____

_____

_____

_____

Tonight I will pray for:

Because:

_____

_____

_____

_____

More about my day:

_____

_____

_____

_____

Today is:_____

The best part of my day was:

_____

_____

_____

_____

Something nice I did for someone today was:

_____

_____

_____

_____

Tonight I will pray for:

Because:

_____

_____

_____

_____

More about my day:

_____

_____

_____

_____

_____

Today is:_____

The best part of my day was:

_____

_____

_____

_____

Something nice I did for someone today was:

_____

_____

_____

_____

Tonight I will pray for:

Because:

_____

_____

_____

_____

More about my day:

_____

_____

_____

_____

The best part of my day was:

_____

_____

_____

_____

Something nice I did for someone today was:

_____

_____

_____

_____

Tonight I will pray for:

Because:

_____

_____

_____

_____

More about my day:

_____

_____

_____

_____

_____

Today is:_____

The best part of my day was:

_____

_____

_____

_____

Something nice I did for someone today was:

_____

_____

_____

_____

Tonight I will pray for:

Because:

_____

_____

_____

_____

More about my day:

_____

_____

_____

_____

_____

Today is:_____

The best part of my day was:

_____

_____

_____

_____

Something nice I did for someone today was:

_____

_____

_____

_____

Tonight I will pray for:

Because:

_____

_____

_____

_____

More about my day:

_____

_____

_____

_____

_____

Today is:_____

The best part of my day was:

_____

_____

_____

_____

Something nice I did for someone today was:

_____

_____

_____

_____

Tonight I will pray for:

Because:

_____

_____

_____

_____

More about my day:

_____

_____

_____

_____

Today is:_____

The best part of my day was:

_____

_____

_____

_____

Something nice I did for someone today was:

_____

_____

_____

_____

Tonight I will pray for:

Because:

_____

_____

_____

_____

More about my day:

_____

_____

_____

_____

_____

Today is:_____

The best part of my day was:

_____

_____

_____

_____

Something nice I did for someone today was:

_____

_____

_____

_____

Tonight I will pray for:

Because:

_____

_____

_____

_____

More about my day:

_____

_____

_____

_____

Today is:_____

The best part of my day was:

_____

_____

_____

_____

Something nice I did for someone today was:

_____

_____

_____

_____

Tonight I will pray for:

Because:

_____

_____

_____

_____

More about my day:

_____

_____

_____

_____

_____

Today is:_____

The best part of my day was:

_____

_____

_____

_____

Something nice I did for someone today was:

_____

_____

_____

_____

Tonight I will pray for:

Because:

_____

_____

_____

_____

More about my day:

_____

_____

_____

_____

Today is:_____

The best part of my day was:

_____

_____

_____

_____

Something nice I did for someone today was:

_____

_____

_____

_____

Tonight I will pray for:

Because:

_____

_____

_____

_____

More about my day:

_____

_____

_____

_____

_____

Today is:_____

The best part of my day was:

_____

_____

_____

_____

Something nice I did for someone today was:

_____

_____

_____

_____

Tonight I will pray for:

Because:

_____

_____

_____

_____

More about my day:

_____

_____

_____

_____

Today is:_____

The best part of my day was:

_____

_____

_____

_____

Something nice I did for someone today was:

_____

_____

_____

_____

Tonight I will pray for:

Because:

_____

_____

_____

_____

More about my day:

_____

_____

_____

_____

_____

Today is:_____

The best part of my day was:

_____

_____

_____

_____

Something nice I did for someone today was:

_____

_____

_____

_____

Tonight I will pray for:

Because:

_____

_____

_____

_____

More about my day:

_____

_____

_____

_____

Today is:_____

The best part of my day was:

_____

_____

_____

_____

Something nice I did for someone today was:

_____

_____

_____

_____

Tonight I will pray for:

Because:

_____

_____

_____

_____

More about my day:

_____

_____

_____

_____

_____

Today is:_____

The best part of my day was:

_____

_____

_____

_____

Something nice I did for someone today was:

_____

_____

_____

_____

Tonight I will pray for:

Because:

_____

_____

_____

_____

More about my day:

_____

_____

_____

_____

Today is:_____

The best part of my day was:

_____

_____

_____

_____

Something nice I did for someone today was:

_____

_____

_____

_____

Tonight I will pray for:

Because:

_____

_____

_____

_____

More about my day:

_____

_____

_____

_____

Today is:_____

The best part of my day was:

_____

_____

_____

_____

Something nice I did for someone today was:

_____

_____

_____

_____

Tonight I will pray for:
Because:

_____

_____

_____

_____

More about my day:

_____

_____

_____

_____

Today is:_____

The best part of my day was:

_____

_____

_____

_____

Something nice I did for someone today was:

_____

_____

_____

_____

Tonight I will pray for:

Because:

_____

_____

_____

_____

More about my day:

_____

_____

_____

_____

_____

Today is:_____

The best part of my day was:

_____

_____

_____

_____

Something nice I did for someone today was:

_____

_____

_____

_____

Tonight I will pray for:

Because:

_____

_____

_____

_____

More about my day:

_____

_____

_____

_____

_____

Today is:_____

The best part of my day was:

_____

_____

_____

_____

Something nice I did for someone today was:

_____

_____

_____

_____

Tonight I will pray for:

Because:

_____

_____

_____

_____

More about my day:

_____

_____

_____

_____

_____

Today is:_____

The best part of my day was:

_____

_____

_____

_____

Something nice I did for someone today was:

_____

_____

_____

_____

Tonight I will pray for:

Because:

_____

_____

_____

_____

More about my day:

_____

_____

_____

_____

_____

Today is:_____

The best part of my day was:

_____

_____

_____

_____

Something nice I did for someone today was:

_____

_____

_____

_____

Tonight I will pray for:

Because:

_____

_____

_____

_____

More about my day:

_____

_____

_____

_____

_____

Today is:_____

The best part of my day was:

_____

_____

_____

_____

Something nice I did for someone today was:

_____

_____

_____

_____

Tonight I will pray for:

Because:

_____

_____

_____

_____

More about my day:

_____

_____

_____

_____

Today is:_____

The best part of my day was:

_____

_____

_____

_____

Something nice I did for someone today was:

_____

_____

_____

_____

Tonight I will pray for:

Because:

_____

_____

_____

_____

More about my day:

_____

_____

_____

_____

_____

Today is:_____

The best part of my day was:

_____

_____

_____

_____

Something nice I did for someone today was:

_____

_____

_____

_____

Tonight I will pray for:

Because:

_____

_____

_____

_____

More about my day:

_____

_____

_____

_____

Today is:_____

The best part of my day was:

_____

_____

_____

_____

Something nice I did for someone today was:

_____

_____

_____

_____

Tonight I will pray for:

Because:

_____

_____

_____

_____

More about my day:

_____

_____

_____

_____

_____

Today is:_____

The best part of my day was:

_____

_____

_____

_____

Something nice I did for someone today was:

_____

_____

_____

_____

Tonight I will pray for:

Because:

_____

_____

_____

_____

More about my day:

_____

_____

_____

_____

Today is:_____

The best part of my day was:

_____

_____

_____

_____

Something nice I did for someone today was:

_____

_____

_____

_____

Tonight I will pray for:

Because:

_____

_____

_____

_____

More about my day:

_____

_____

_____

_____

_____

Today is:_____

The best part of my day was:

_____

_____

_____

_____

Something nice I did for someone today was:

_____

_____

_____

_____

Tonight I will pray for:

Because:

_____

_____

_____

_____

More about my day:

_____

_____

_____

_____

Today is:_____

The best part of my day was:

_____

_____

_____

_____

Something nice I did for someone today was:

_____

_____

_____

_____

Tonight I will pray for:

Because:

_____

_____

_____

_____

More about my day:

_____

_____

_____

_____

_____

Today is:_____

The best part of my day was:

_____

_____

_____

_____

Something nice I did for someone today was:

_____

_____

_____

_____

Tonight I will pray for:

Because:

_____

_____

_____

_____

More about my day:

_____

_____

_____

_____

Today is:_____

The best part of my day was:

_____

_____

_____

_____

Something nice I did for someone today was:

_____

_____

_____

_____

Tonight I will pray for:

Because:

_____

_____

_____

_____

More about my day:

_____

_____

_____

_____

_____

Today is:_____

The best part of my day was:

_____

_____

_____

_____

Something nice I did for someone today was:

_____

_____

_____

_____

Tonight I will pray for:

Because:

_____

_____

_____

_____

More about my day:

_____

_____

_____

_____

Today is:_____

The best part of my day was:

_____

_____

_____

_____

Something nice I did for someone today was:

_____

_____

_____

_____

Tonight I will pray for:

Because:

_____

_____

_____

_____

More about my day:

_____

_____

_____

_____

_____

Today is:_____

The best part of my day was:

_____

_____

_____

_____

Something nice I did for someone today was:

_____

_____

_____

_____

Tonight I will pray for:

Because:

_____

_____

_____

_____

More about my day:

_____

_____

_____

_____

Today is:_____

The best part of my day was:

_____

_____

_____

_____

Something nice I did for someone today was:

_____

_____

_____

_____

Tonight I will pray for:

Because:

_____

_____

_____

_____

More about my day:

_____

_____

_____

_____

_____

Today is:_____

The best part of my day was:

_____

_____

_____

_____

Something nice I did for someone today was:

_____

_____

_____

_____

Tonight I will pray for:

Because:

_____

_____

_____

_____

More about my day:

_____

_____

_____

_____

Today is:_____

The best part of my day was:

_____

_____

_____

_____

Something nice I did for someone today was:

_____

_____

_____

_____

Tonight I will pray for:

Because:

_____

_____

_____

_____

More about my day:

_____

_____

_____

_____

_____

Today is:_____

The best part of my day was:

_____

_____

_____

_____

Something nice I did for someone today was:

_____

_____

_____

_____

Tonight I will pray for:

Because:

_____

_____

_____

_____

More about my day:

_____

_____

_____

_____

Today is:_____

The best part of my day was:

_____

_____

_____

_____

Something nice I did for someone today was:

_____

_____

_____

_____

Tonight I will pray for:

Because:

_____

_____

_____

_____

More about my day:

_____

_____

_____

_____

_____

Today is:_____

The best part of my day was:

_____

_____

_____

_____

Something nice I did for someone today was:

_____

_____

_____

_____

Tonight I will pray for:

Because:

_____

_____

_____

_____

More about my day:

_____

_____

_____

_____

_____

Today is:_____

The best part of my day was:

_____

_____

_____

_____

Something nice I did for someone today was:

_____

_____

_____

_____

Tonight I will pray for:

Because:

_____

_____

_____

_____

More about my day:

_____

_____

_____

_____

_____

Today is:_____

The best part of my day was:

_____
_____
_____
_____

Something nice I did for someone today was:

_____
_____
_____
_____

Tonight I will pray for:

Because:

_____
_____
_____
_____

More about my day:

_____
_____
_____
_____

Today is:_____

The best part of my day was:

_____

_____

_____

_____

Something nice I did for someone today was:

_____

_____

_____

_____

Tonight I will pray for:

Because:

_____

_____

_____

_____

More about my day:

_____

_____

_____

_____

Today is:_____

The best part of my day was:

_____

_____

_____

_____

Something nice I did for someone today was:

_____

_____

_____

_____

Tonight I will pray for:

Because:

_____

_____

_____

_____

More about my day:

_____

_____

_____

_____

_____

Today is:_____

The best part of my day was:

_____

_____

_____

_____

Something nice I did for someone today was:

_____

_____

_____

_____

Tonight I will pray for:

Because:

_____

_____

_____

_____

More about my day:

_____

_____

_____

_____

Today is:_____

The best part of my day was:

_____

_____

_____

_____

Something nice I did for someone today was:

_____

_____

_____

_____

Tonight I will pray for:

Because:

_____

_____

_____

_____

More about my day:

_____

_____

_____

_____

_____

Today is:_____

The best part of my day was:

_____

_____

_____

_____

Something nice I did for someone today was:

_____

_____

_____

_____

Tonight I will pray for:

Because:

_____

_____

_____

_____

More about my day:

_____

_____

_____

_____

_____

Today is:_____

The best part of my day was:

_____

_____

_____

_____

Something nice I did for someone today was:

_____

_____

_____

_____

Tonight I will pray for:

Because:

_____

_____

_____

_____

More about my day:

_____

_____

_____

_____

_____

Today is:_____

The best part of my day was:

_____

_____

_____

_____

Something nice I did for someone today was:

_____

_____

_____

_____

Tonight I will pray for:

Because:

_____

_____

_____

_____

More about my day:

_____

_____

_____

_____

_____

Today is:_____

The best part of my day was:

_____

_____

_____

_____

Something nice I did for someone today was:

_____

_____

_____

_____

Tonight I will pray for:

Because:

_____

_____

_____

_____

More about my day:

_____

_____

_____

_____

_____

Today is:_____

The best part of my day was:

_____

_____

_____

_____

Something nice I did for someone today was:

_____

_____

_____

_____

Tonight I will pray for:

Because:

_____

_____

_____

_____

More about my day:

_____

_____

_____

_____

_____

Today is:_____

The best part of my day was:

_____

_____

_____

_____

Something nice I did for someone today was:

_____

_____

_____

_____

Tonight I will pray for:
Because:

_____

_____

_____

_____

More about my day:

_____

_____

_____

_____

Today is:_____

The best part of my day was:

_____

_____

_____

_____

Something nice I did for someone today was:

_____

_____

_____

_____

Tonight I will pray for:

Because:

_____

_____

_____

_____

More about my day:

_____

_____

_____

_____

Today is:_____

The best part of my day was:

_____

_____

_____

_____

Something nice I did for someone today was:

_____

_____

_____

_____

Tonight I will pray for:

Because:

_____

_____

_____

_____

More about my day:

_____

_____

_____

_____

_____

Today is:_____

The best part of my day was:

_____

_____

_____

_____

Something nice I did for someone today was:

_____

_____

_____

_____

Tonight I will pray for:

Because:

_____

_____

_____

_____

More about my day:

_____

_____

_____

_____

_____

Today is:_____

The best part of my day was:

_____

_____

_____

_____

Something nice I did for someone today was:

_____

_____

_____

_____

Tonight I will pray for:
Because:

_____

_____

_____

_____

More about my day:

_____

_____

_____

_____

_____

Today is:_____

The best part of my day was:

_____

_____

_____

_____

Something nice I did for someone today was:

_____

_____

_____

_____

Tonight I will pray for:

Because:

_____

_____

_____

_____

More about my day:

_____

_____

_____

_____

_____

Today is:_____

The best part of my day was:

_____

_____

_____

_____

Something nice I did for someone today was:

_____

_____

_____

_____

Tonight I will pray for:

Because:

_____

_____

_____

_____

More about my day:

_____

_____

_____

_____

Today is:_____

The best part of my day was:

_____

_____

_____

_____

Something nice I did for someone today was:

_____

_____

_____

_____

Tonight I will pray for:

Because:

_____

_____

_____

_____

More about my day:

_____

_____

_____

_____

_____

Today is:_____

The best part of my day was:

_____

_____

_____

_____

Something nice I did for someone today was:

_____

_____

_____

_____

Tonight I will pray for:

Because:

_____

_____

_____

_____

More about my day:

_____

_____

_____

_____

_____

Today is:_____

The best part of my day was:

_____

_____

_____

_____

Something nice I did for someone today was:

_____

_____

_____

_____

Tonight I will pray for:

Because:

_____

_____

_____

_____

More about my day:

_____

_____

_____

_____

_____

Today is:_____

The best part of my day was:

_____

_____

_____

_____

Something nice I did for someone today was:

_____

_____

_____

_____

Tonight I will pray for:

Because:

_____

_____

_____

_____

More about my day:

_____

_____

_____

_____

Today is:_____

The best part of my day was:

_____

_____

_____

_____

Something nice I did for someone today was:

_____

_____

_____

_____

Tonight I will pray for:

Because:

_____

_____

_____

_____

More about my day:

_____

_____

_____

_____

Today is:_____

The best part of my day was:

_____

_____

_____

_____

Something nice I did for someone today was:

_____

_____

_____

_____

Tonight I will pray for:

Because:

_____

_____

_____

_____

More about my day:

_____

_____

_____

_____

Today is:_____

The best part of my day was:

_____

_____

_____

_____

Something nice I did for someone today was:

_____

_____

_____

_____

Tonight I will pray for:
Because:

_____

_____

_____

_____

More about my day:

_____

_____

_____

_____

Today is:_____

The best part of my day was:

_____

_____

_____

_____

Something nice I did for someone today was:

_____

_____

_____

_____

Tonight I will pray for:

Because:

_____

_____

_____

_____

More about my day:

_____

_____

_____

_____

_____

Today is:_____

The best part of my day was:

_____

_____

_____

_____

Something nice I did for someone today was:

_____

_____

_____

_____

Tonight I will pray for:

Because:

_____

_____

_____

_____

More about my day:

_____

_____

_____

_____

_____

Today is:_____

The best part of my day was:

_____

_____

_____

_____

Something nice I did for someone today was:

_____

_____

_____

_____

Tonight I will pray for:

Because:

_____

_____

_____

_____

More about my day:

_____

_____

_____

_____

_____

Today is:_____

The best part of my day was:

_____

_____

_____

_____

Something nice I did for someone today was:

_____

_____

_____

_____

Tonight I will pray for:

Because:

_____

_____

_____

_____

More about my day:

_____

_____

_____

_____

Today is:_____

The best part of my day was:

_____

_____

_____

_____

Something nice I did for someone today was:

_____

_____

_____

_____

Tonight I will pray for:

Because:

_____

_____

_____

_____

More about my day:

_____

_____

_____

_____

Today is:_____

The best part of my day was:

_____

_____

_____

_____

Something nice I did for someone today was:

_____

_____

_____

_____

Tonight I will pray for:
Because:

_____

_____

_____

_____

More about my day:

_____

_____

_____

_____

Today is:_____

The best part of my day was:

_____

_____

_____

_____

Something nice I did for someone today was:

_____

_____

_____

_____

Tonight I will pray for:

Because:

_____

_____

_____

_____

More about my day:

_____

_____

_____

_____

Today is:_____

The best part of my day was:

_____

_____

_____

_____

Something nice I did for someone today was:

_____

_____

_____

_____

Tonight I will pray for:

Because:

_____

_____

_____

_____

More about my day:

_____

_____

_____

_____

_____

Today is:_____

The best part of my day was:

_____

_____

_____

_____

Something nice I did for someone today was:

_____

_____

_____

_____

Tonight I will pray for:
Because:

_____

_____

_____

_____

More about my day:

_____

_____

_____

_____

Today is:_____

The best part of my day was:

_____

_____

_____

_____

Something nice I did for someone today was:

_____

_____

_____

_____

Tonight I will pray for:

Because:

_____

_____

_____

_____

More about my day:

_____

_____

_____

_____

_____

Today is:_____

The best part of my day was:

_____

_____

_____

_____

Something nice I did for someone today was:

_____

_____

_____

_____

Tonight I will pray for:

Because:

_____

_____

_____

_____

More about my day:

_____

_____

_____

_____

_____

Today is:_____

The best part of my day was:

_____

_____

_____

_____

Something nice I did for someone today was:

_____

_____

_____

_____

Tonight I will pray for:

Because:

_____

_____

_____

_____

More about my day:

_____

_____

_____

_____

Today is:_____

The best part of my day was:

_____

_____

_____

_____

Something nice I did for someone today was:

_____

_____

_____

_____

Tonight I will pray for:

Because:

_____

_____

_____

_____

More about my day:

_____

_____

_____

_____

_____

Today is:_____

The best part of my day was:

_____

_____

_____

_____

Something nice I did for someone today was:

_____

_____

_____

_____

Tonight I will pray for:

Because:

_____

_____

_____

_____

More about my day:

_____

_____

_____

_____

_____

Today is:_____

The best part of my day was:

_____

_____

_____

_____

Something nice I did for someone today was:

_____

_____

_____

_____

Tonight I will pray for:

Because:

_____

_____

_____

_____

More about my day:

_____

_____

_____

_____

_____

Today is:_____

The best part of my day was:

_____

_____

_____

_____

Something nice I did for someone today was:

_____

_____

_____

_____

Tonight I will pray for:

Because:

_____

_____

_____

_____

More about my day:

_____

_____

_____

_____

_____

Today is:_____

The best part of my day was:

_____

_____

_____

_____

Something nice I did for someone today was:

_____

_____

_____

_____

Tonight I will pray for:

Because:

_____

_____

_____

_____

More about my day:

_____

_____

_____

_____

Today is:_____

The best part of my day was:

_____

_____

_____

_____

Something nice I did for someone today was:

_____

_____

_____

_____

Tonight I will pray for:

Because:

_____

_____

_____

_____

More about my day:

_____

_____

_____

_____

_____

Today is:_____

The best part of my day was:

_____

_____

_____

_____

Something nice I did for someone today was:

_____

_____

_____

_____

Tonight I will pray for:
Because:

_____

_____

_____

_____

More about my day:

_____

_____

_____

_____

_____

Today is:_____

The best part of my day was:

_____

_____

_____

_____

Something nice I did for someone today was:

_____

_____

_____

_____

Tonight I will pray for:

Because:

_____

_____

_____

_____

More about my day:

_____

_____

_____

_____

_____

Today is:_____

The best part of my day was:

_____

_____

_____

_____

Something nice I did for someone today was:

_____

_____

_____

_____

Tonight I will pray for:
Because:

_____

_____

_____

_____

More about my day:

_____

_____

_____

_____

Today is:_____

The best part of my day was:

_____

_____

_____

_____

Something nice I did for someone today was:

_____

_____

_____

_____

Tonight I will pray for:

Because:

_____

_____

_____

_____

More about my day:

_____

_____

_____

_____

_____

Today is:_____

The best part of my day was:

_____

_____

_____

_____

Something nice I did for someone today was:

_____

_____

_____

_____

Tonight I will pray for:

Because:

_____

_____

_____

_____

More about my day:

_____

_____

_____

_____

_____

Today is:_____

The best part of my day was:

_____

_____

_____

_____

Something nice I did for someone today was:

_____

_____

_____

_____

Tonight I will pray for:

Because:

_____

_____

_____

_____

More about my day:

_____

_____

_____

_____

_____

Today is:_____

The best part of my day was:

_____

_____

_____

_____

Something nice I did for someone today was:

_____

_____

_____

_____

Tonight I will pray for:
Because:

_____

_____

_____

_____

More about my day:

_____

_____

_____

_____

_____

Today is:_____

The best part of my day was:

_____

_____

_____

_____

Something nice I did for someone today was:

_____

_____

_____

_____

Tonight I will pray for:

Because:

_____

_____

_____

_____

More about my day:

_____

_____

_____

_____

_____

Today is:_____

The best part of my day was:

_____

_____

_____

_____

Something nice I did for someone today was:

_____

_____

_____

_____

Tonight I will pray for:

Because:

_____

_____

_____

_____

More about my day:

_____

_____

_____

_____

Today is:_____

The best part of my day was:

_____

_____

_____

_____

Something nice I did for someone today was:

_____

_____

_____

_____

Tonight I will pray for:

Because:

_____

_____

_____

_____

More about my day:

_____

_____

_____

_____

Today is:_____

The best part of my day was:

_____

_____

_____

_____

Something nice I did for someone today was:

_____

_____

_____

_____

Tonight I will pray for:
Because:

_____

_____

_____

_____

More about my day:

_____

_____

_____

_____

_____

Today is:_____

The best part of my day was:

_____

_____

_____

_____

Something nice I did for someone today was:

_____

_____

_____

_____

Tonight I will pray for:

Because:

_____

_____

_____

_____

More about my day:

_____

_____

_____

_____

_____

Today is:_____

The best part of my day was:

_____

_____

_____

_____

Something nice I did for someone today was:

_____

_____

_____

_____

Tonight I will pray for:
Because:

_____

_____

_____

_____

More about my day:

_____

_____

_____

_____

Today is:_____

The best part of my day was:

_____

_____

_____

_____

Something nice I did for someone today was:

_____

_____

_____

_____

Tonight I will pray for:

Because:

_____

_____

_____

_____

More about my day:

_____

_____

_____

_____

_____

Today is:_____

The best part of my day was:

_____

_____

_____

_____

Something nice I did for someone today was:

_____

_____

_____

_____

Tonight I will pray for:

Because:

_____

_____

_____

_____

More about my day:

_____

_____

_____

_____

Today is:_____

The best part of my day was:

_____

_____

_____

_____

Something nice I did for someone today was:

_____

_____

_____

_____

Tonight I will pray for:
Because:

_____

_____

_____

_____

More about my day:

_____

_____

_____

_____

Today is:_____

The best part of my day was:

_____

_____

_____

_____

Something nice I did for someone today was:

_____

_____

_____

_____

Tonight I will pray for:
Because:

_____

_____

_____

_____

More about my day:

_____

_____

_____

_____

Today is:_____

The best part of my day was:

_____

_____

_____

_____

Something nice I did for someone today was:

_____

_____

_____

_____

Tonight I will pray for:

Because:

_____

_____

_____

_____

More about my day:

_____

_____

_____

_____

_____

Today is:_____

The best part of my day was:

_____

_____

_____

_____

Something nice I did for someone today was:

_____

_____

_____

_____

Tonight I will pray for:

Because:

_____

_____

_____

_____

More about my day:

_____

_____

_____

_____

_____

Today is:_____

The best part of my day was:

_____

_____

_____

_____

Something nice I did for someone today was:

_____

_____

_____

_____

Tonight I will pray for:

Because:

_____

_____

_____

_____

More about my day:

_____

_____

_____

_____

_____

Today is:_____

The best part of my day was:

_____

_____

_____

_____

Something nice I did for someone today was:

_____

_____

_____

_____

Tonight I will pray for:
Because:

_____

_____

_____

_____

More about my day:

_____

_____

_____

_____

Today is:_____

The best part of my day was:

_____

_____

_____

_____

Something nice I did for someone today was:

_____

_____

_____

_____

Tonight I will pray for:

Because:

_____

_____

_____

_____

More about my day:

_____

_____

_____

_____

_____

Today is:_____

The best part of my day was:

_____

_____

_____

_____

Something nice I did for someone today was:

_____

_____

_____

_____

Tonight I will pray for:

Because:

_____

_____

_____

_____

More about my day:

_____

_____

_____

_____

_____

Today is:_____

The best part of my day was:

_____

_____

_____

_____

Something nice I did for someone today was:

_____

_____

_____

_____

Tonight I will pray for:

Because:

_____

_____

_____

_____

More about my day:

_____

_____

_____

_____

_____

Today is:_____

The best part of my day was:

_____

_____

_____

_____

Something nice I did for someone today was:

_____

_____

_____

_____

Tonight I will pray for:
Because:

_____

_____

_____

_____

More about my day:

_____

_____

_____

_____

_____

Today is:_____

The best part of my day was:

_____

_____

_____

_____

Something nice I did for someone today was:

_____

_____

_____

_____

Tonight I will pray for:

Because:

_____

_____

_____

_____

More about my day:

_____

_____

_____

_____

Today is:_____

The best part of my day was:

_____

_____

_____

_____

Something nice I did for someone today was:

_____

_____

_____

_____

Tonight I will pray for:

Because:

_____

_____

_____

_____

More about my day:

_____

_____

_____

_____

Today is:_____

The best part of my day was:

_____

_____

_____

_____

Something nice I did for someone today was:

_____

_____

_____

_____

Tonight I will pray for:

Because:

_____

_____

_____

_____

More about my day:

_____

_____

_____

_____

_____

Today is:_____

The best part of my day was:

_____

_____

_____

_____

Something nice I did for someone today was:

_____

_____

_____

_____

Tonight I will pray for:

Because:

_____

_____

_____

_____

More about my day:

_____

_____

_____

_____

_____

Today is:_____

The best part of my day was:

_____

_____

_____

_____

Something nice I did for someone today was:

_____

_____

_____

_____

Tonight I will pray for:

Because:

_____

_____

_____

_____

More about my day:

_____

_____

_____

_____

_____

Today is:_____

The best part of my day was:

_____

_____

_____

_____

Something nice I did for someone today was:

_____

_____

_____

_____

Tonight I will pray for:

Because:

_____

_____

_____

_____

More about my day:

_____

_____

_____

_____

Today is:_____

The best part of my day was:

_____

_____

_____

_____

Something nice I did for someone today was:

_____

_____

_____

_____

Tonight I will pray for:

Because:

_____

_____

_____

_____

More about my day:

_____

_____

_____

_____

Today is:_____

The best part of my day was:

_____

_____

_____

_____

Something nice I did for someone today was:

_____

_____

_____

_____

Tonight I will pray for:
Because:

_____

_____

_____

_____

More about my day:

_____

_____

_____

_____

_____

Today is:_____

The best part of my day was:

_____

_____

_____

_____

Something nice I did for someone today was:

_____

_____

_____

_____

Tonight I will pray for:

Because:

_____

_____

_____

_____

More about my day:

_____

_____

_____

_____

Today is:_____

The best part of my day was:

_____

_____

_____

_____

Something nice I did for someone today was:

_____

_____

_____

_____

Tonight I will pray for:

Because:

_____

_____

_____

_____

More about my day:

_____

_____

_____

_____

_____

Today is:_____

The best part of my day was:

_____

_____

_____

_____

Something nice I did for someone today was:

_____

_____

_____

_____

Tonight I will pray for:

Because:

_____

_____

_____

_____

More about my day:

_____

_____

_____

_____

_____

Today is:_____

The best part of my day was:

_____

_____

_____

_____

Something nice I did for someone today was:

_____

_____

_____

_____

Tonight I will pray for:
Because:

_____

_____

_____

_____

More about my day:

_____

_____

_____

_____

Today is:_____

The best part of my day was:

_____

_____

_____

_____

Something nice I did for someone today was:

_____

_____

_____

_____

Tonight I will pray for:

Because:

_____

_____

_____

_____

More about my day:

_____

_____

_____

_____

_____

Today is:_____

The best part of my day was:

_____

_____

_____

_____

Something nice I did for someone today was:

_____

_____

_____

_____

Tonight I will pray for:

Because:

_____

_____

_____

_____

More about my day:

_____

_____

_____

_____

_____

Today is:_____

The best part of my day was:

_____

_____

_____

_____

Something nice I did for someone today was:

_____

_____

_____

_____

Tonight I will pray for:

Because:

_____

_____

_____

_____

More about my day:

_____

_____

_____

_____

_____

Today is:_____

The best part of my day was:

_____

_____

_____

_____

Something nice I did for someone today was:

_____

_____

_____

_____

Tonight I will pray for:

Because:

_____

_____

_____

_____

More about my day:

_____

_____

_____

_____

Today is:_____

The best part of my day was:

_____

_____

_____

_____

Something nice I did for someone today was:

_____

_____

_____

_____

Tonight I will pray for:

Because:

_____

_____

_____

_____

More about my day:

_____

_____

_____

_____

_____

Today is:_____

The best part of my day was:

_____

_____

_____

_____

Something nice I did for someone today was:

_____

_____

_____

_____

Tonight I will pray for:

Because:

_____

_____

_____

_____

More about my day:

_____

_____

_____

_____

Today is:_____

The best part of my day was:

_____

_____

_____

_____

Something nice I did for someone today was:

_____

_____

_____

_____

Tonight I will pray for:

Because:

_____

_____

_____

_____

More about my day:

_____

_____

_____

_____

_____